GETTING STARTED WITH AIRTAGS

AN INSANELY EASY GUIDE TO KEEPING
TRACK OF YOUR THINGS WITH AIRTAG

SCOTT LA COUNTE

RIDICULOUSLY
SIMPLE BOOKS
ANAHEIM, CALIFORNIA

www.RidiculouslySimpleBooks.com

Copyright © 2021 by Scott La Counte.

All rights reserved. No part of this publication may be reproduced, distributed or transmitted in any form or by any means, including photocopying, recording, or other electronic or mechanical methods, without the prior written permission of the publisher, except in the case of brief quotations embodied in critical reviews and certain other noncommercial uses permitted by copyright law.

Limited Liability / Disclaimer of Warranty. While best efforts have been used in preparing this book, the author and publishers make no representations or warranties of any kind and assume no liabilities of any kind with respect to accuracy or completeness of the content and specifically the author nor publisher shall be held liable or responsible to any person or entity with respect to any loss or incidental or consequential damages caused or alleged to have been caused, directly, or indirectly without limitations, by the information or programs contained herein. Furthermore, readers should be aware that the Internet sites listed in this work may have changed or disappeared. This work is sold with the understanding that the advice inside may not be suitable in every situation.

Trademarks. Where trademarks are used in this book this infers no endorsement or any affiliation with this book. Any trademarks (including, but not limiting to, screenshots) used in this book are solely used for editorial and educational purposes.

Table of Contents

Introduction *5*

What AirTag Is (And Isn't) *6*

Setting Up AirTag *9*

    Replacing a Battery 14

Finding Your AirTag *16*

    Lost Mode 23

    Rename Item 26

    Remove Item 27

        Factory Reset Without Bluetooth 28

About the Author *30*

Disclaimer: Please note, while every effort has been made to ensure accuracy, this book is not endorsed by Apple, Inc. and should be considered unofficial.

INTRODUCTION

For years, tracking keys, suitcases, and other valuables could be done with a small tracker—one most likely made by Tile. That's all changed.

Apple announced in Spring 2021 that it was entering the race to find the things you love with the Apple AirTag—a small, puck-shaped device that can help locate keys, bags, and much more.

This short guide will tell you what you need to know about the powerful new tracker.

[1]
What AirTag Is (And Isn't)

As with anything new, many people heard about the tracker and their minds jumped immediately to the possibilities of tracking pets and humans. Because of that, let's address the elephant in the room: AirTags are _not_ meant to track pets or humans.

Apple has publicly said that the best way to keep track of your young children is not through AirTags, but rather Apple Watches.

As with any new technology, there's always that one person who has to be a bit...creepy. So let's talk about that person too. What happens if someone is trying to follow you and they slip an AirTag into your bag? They now are able to remotely follow you and see where you live, right? Yes and no. If the person is an iPhone user, then they'll get a prompt that tells them that it looks like there's an unauthorized tag following them, and they'll be asked if they want to stop the tracking. If they have Android, then after three days, the device will start to ring and assuming it's still nearby, they'll hear it.

One of the most popular things people have said they wanted to track is their cars; hiding your AirTag in your car means you'll always be able to find it when you're at a mall and forget where you parked; and it means if someone's taken your car, you'll know exactly where it's at still (assuming there's another iPhone in range and the person who has taken it doesn't have an iPhone—because they'd be alerted they were being tracked).

And what about pets? While Apple does not suggest using it on pets, there's nothing exactly stopping you. But you have to remember if your pet gets loose, you can only track them if someone else has an iPhone within range of where they are.

How exactly does the device work? Like other trackers, the AirTag relies on a network of devices to track your lost items; in the AirTag's case, it relies on other iPhones. And there are millions and millions of iPhones out there helping you keep track of things. So let's say you are in an airport and you lose your luggage; if you can't find your luggage, then there's a pretty good chance your iPhone isn't anywhere near it—so how will you be able to track it? That's where those millions and millions of other iPhones help out—as long as there's a person with an iPhone near your AirTag, then you'll be able to figure out where the bag is.

So now that you know a little more about it, let's learn a little more about how to use it.

[2]

Setting Up AirTag

To get started, you need either an iPhone (running iOS 14.5 or higher) or an iPad (running iPadOS 14.5 or higher); AirTag is not compatible with Android phones at this writing.

Not surprisingly, the AirTag case, like other Apple products, is pretty minimal. There are a few instructions and the AirTag itself.

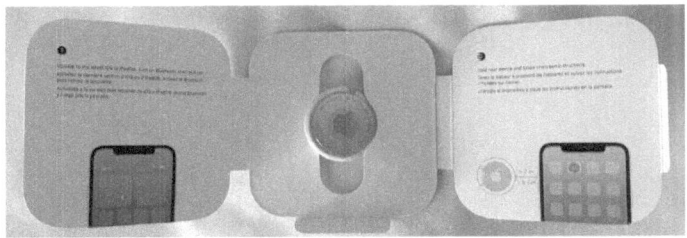

You'll want to pull the AirTag out to pair it; there's a piece of plastic attached to it. That plastic is basically making sure the battery isn't being used. Unlike other Apple products, AirTag uses a disposable battery (it lasts about a year). When you're ready to turn it on, pull the plastic off it. You'll hear a chirp to confirm it's on.

Once you hear the chirp, move the AirTag next to your iPhone (make sure your Bluetooth is turned on)—I found that the best place for it was right next to the Side Button. Once it's next to your phone, it will automatically launch a menu with a button to connect it. Click the "Connect" button.

Next it will ask you to name your AirTag; it will give you all kinds of suggestions (i.e. Backpack, keys, etc.). If you don't see what you want to add or want to name it yourself, then go to the last option and do a custom name. You will be able to rename it later.

If you did the custom option, then add a name and click Continue.

Next pick an emoji for your AirTag; you'll have an item name assigned to it—the emoji just helps you find it quickly on the map.

Finally, you'll see a message saying your AirTag will be assigned to your Apple ID and phone number. If you want this to be someone else's AirTag, then do not finish the setup. They will need to do it on their device.

Next you'll see a spinner confirming that the AirTag is being set up. It will take just a few seconds.

The last screen of the setup will just tell you where to find your item. If you'd like to go there, click the view button; if not, then click the Done option.

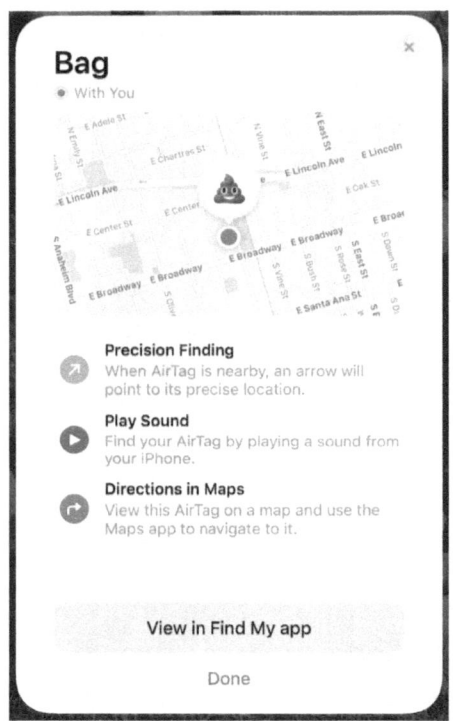

REPLACING A BATTERY

The AirTag's battery will last about a year. But eventually you need to replace it. How will you know? Your phone will warn you it's low. But if it's been about a year, you can also replace it to be safe.

The AirTag takes a CR2032 battery.

If you are ready to get the battery out, turn the AirTag silver side up. Next, press down on the silver casing with both of your thumbs and turn counterclockwise. Keep turning until it's loose enough to remove the halves. Take the battery out and replace it with a CR2032 with the positive (+) side facing up. Put the top cover back on and rotate it clockwise. You should hear your AirTag make a chime.

[3]
FINDING YOUR AIRTAG

When you're ready to find your lost or misplaced item, open the Find Now app. While you cannot set up the AirTag on a MacBook, you can view it. These steps will apply to iPhone, iPad, and Mac—the screens are just sized slightly differently.

If you are not familiar with the Find My app, you should be! It's a powerful little app—it lets you find not only your lost or stolen devices (from AirPods to iPhones), it lets you find people! As an example, I have permission to track members in my immediate family, so if I am concerned about where they are, I am one app away from finding them.

When you open the app, the first thing you see is Devices, which is a little confusing, because isn't the AirTag one of your devices? Yes and no...but for the sake of this app, no.

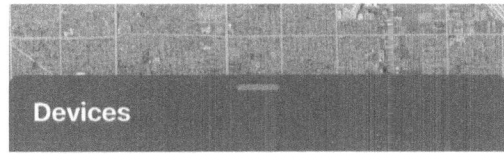

To find your AirTag, click the Items button on the bottom menu.

When you tap Items, you'll see where the AirTag currently is; to find it, you'll tap on the round emoji on the map. This brings up a new menu. You can either tap Play Sound to make it make a noise to find an item, or you can tap Find to bring up a compass-like navigation. For this book, I'll show you how to find it using the compass type navigation, so tap Find.

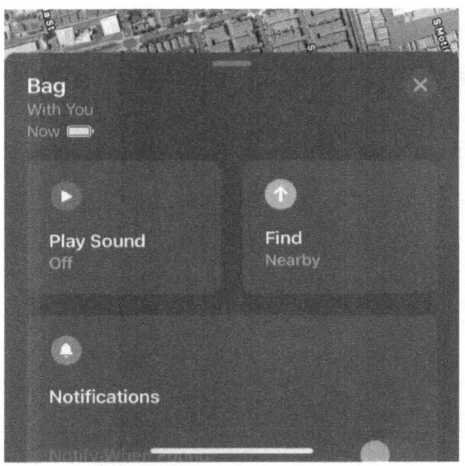

Assuming you are nearby the item, you'll get an arrow that points you to where it is and how far away it is. You can also tap the sound icon in the lower right corner to make it start chiming.

The color of your screen will turn to green as you get closer.

When you are practically on top of it, all you'll see is a circle—no arrows. You'll also feel a slight haptic vibration on your phone to indicate you are near it.

This is all great...but what happens if you aren't by the device? You will still see the approximate address of where the AirTag is, but you'll see one of two messages:

A message saying "Searching for signal. Try moving to a different location." That means there is no phone or device close enough to it to pinpoint it (remember, it relies on other iPhone or iPad devices to find it).

A message saying "Connected. Signal is weak. Try moving to a different location." That means you are a few feet from it, but not close enough to pinpoint it. If you see that message, then just try moving to another area of the room and waiting a second to see if that fixes it.

Once the device has been found, just tap the X button to close the navigation. This returns you to the previous screen.

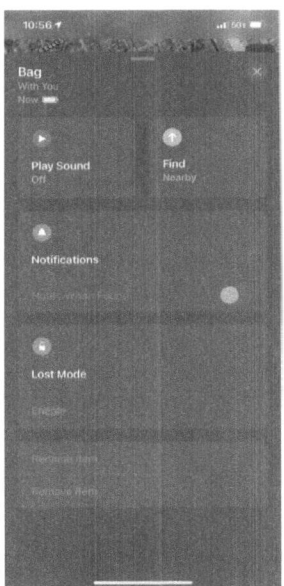

LOST MODE

If the unthinkable happens and you lose your item, then you'll quickly learn why this is the best $29 you ever spent! Open the Find Now app, and tap the Enable button under Lost Mode.

To start the mode, tap the Continue button.

What happens now? Few things:

One, nobody is going to be able to use that AirTag. Ever. It's tied to your account, so you don't have to worry about someone stealing it and then pairing it to their own account.

Two, you will be able to leave a message with how to contact you.

Three, when the device is in range of another iPhone, it will tell the user it is near a lost AirTag and let them know how to reach out.

When you tap continue, the first thing it will ask is for your phone number. You don't have to use your device's phone number. So if you are worried about your piracy, you could use something like a Google Number. Tap Next in the upper right corner to continue.

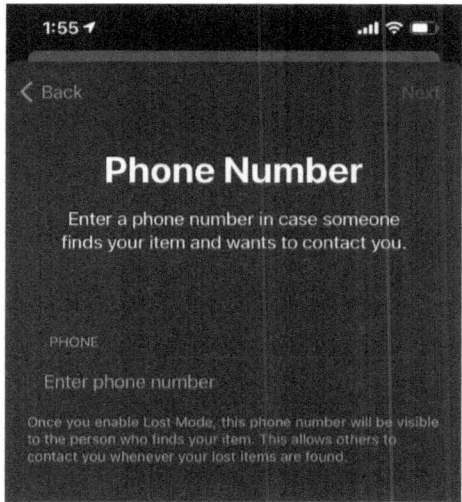

On the next screen, you can either have the default message, or add in a personal one. Tap Activate in the upper right corner when you are ready to turn Lost Mode on.

To turn off Lost Mode, go to Turn Off from the main AirTag screen, and tap Turn Off Lost Mode.

RENAME ITEM

If you decide the AirTag you have in your bag should really go on your remote (or anywhere else), then tap Rename from your main Items menu. You can add a custom name or use a pre-generated name. Tapping on the emoji lets you select a different emoji for the AirTag as well. So if you only want to change the emoji, you will still go to Rename.

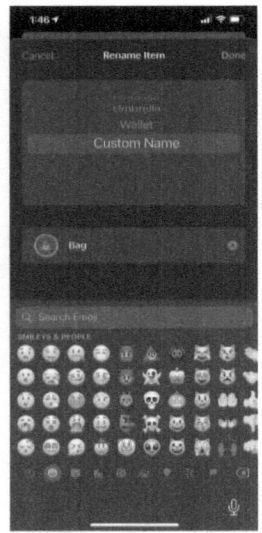

Remove Item

If you decide AirTag isn't right for you, or you prefer it be tied to someone else's account, then go to the Remove button on your main Items menu. This will remove it from your account, so another person can use it. They will need to set it up as if it's a brand new AirTag.

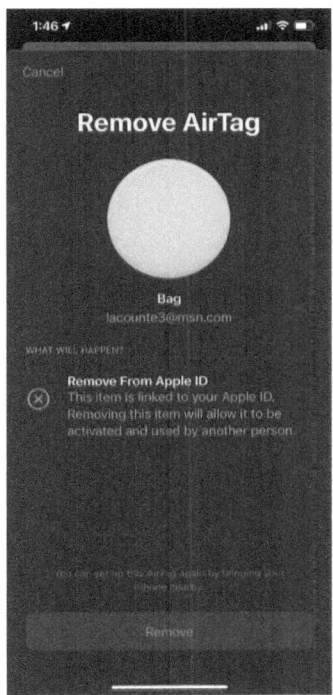

Factory Reset Without Bluetooth

Resetting your AirTag is great...when it's next to you. Before I explain, let me first say this: make sure it's in range before you remove it! It's going to be a lot easier for you if you don't do it manually.

But what about when it's not in range when you remove it? You'll need to do a manual reset.

If that happened to you, press down on the stainless backing of the AirTag, then, as you are still pressing down, rotate it counterclockwise. Keep rotating iti until it stops, then pull apart the two halves and take out the battery.

After you remove the battery, put it back in and press down on it until you hear a sound. Keep pressing until the sound finishes.

Repeat this four times (i.e. remove battery, put it back in, wait for sound). You need to hear that sound five times total. It's not reset until you do it a total of five times.

Once your done, put the other cover on and align the three tabbed slots, then press down on the cover until there's a sound and rotate it until it is locked in place.

ABOUT THE AUTHOR

Scott La Counte is a librarian and writer. His first book, *Quiet, Please: Dispatches from a Public Librarian* (Da Capo 2008) was the editor's choice for the Chicago Tribune and a Discovery title for the Los Angeles Times; in 2011, he published the YA book The N00b Warriors, which became a #1 Amazon bestseller; his most recent book is *#OrganicJesus: Finding Your Way to an Unprocessed, GMO-Free Christianity* (Kregel 2016).

He has written dozens of best-selling how-to guides on tech products.

You can connect with him at ScottDouglas.org.

www.ingramcontent.com/pod-product-compliance
Lightning Source LLC
Chambersburg PA
CBHW031517210526
45464CB00007B/2954